ECO-DISASTERS

TOXIC WATER

MINAMATA, JAPAN

by Meish Goldish

Consultant: September Williams, MD
Writer and Bioethicist

BEARPORT
PUBLISHING

New York, New York

Credits

Cover and Title Page, © Jsunphoto/Shutterstock; 4T, © Charles Gorry/AP Photo; 4B, © JTB MEDIA CREATION, Inc./Alamy; 6, © Noko3/Shutterstock; 7L, © suatcan/Shutterstock; 7TR, © Akvdanil/Dreamstime; 7BR, © Chad Zuber/Shutterstock; 8T, © hikariphoto/Fotolia; 8B, © Kamonchanok Changsomboon/Shutterstock; 9, © Kyodo via AP Images; 10, © Mint Images Limited/Alamy; 11T, © HUANSHENG XU/Shutterstock; 11B, © Science History Images/Alamy; 12, © JTB MEDIA CREATION, Inc./Alamy; 13, © Takeshi Ishikawa/Polaris; 14, © David Guttenfelder/AP Photo; 15, © jeremy sutton-hibbert/Alamy; 16, © David Guttenfelder/AP Photo; 17T, © Kyodo/Newscom; 17B, © Kyodo/Newscom; 18, © AP Photo; 19T, © Kyodo via AP Images; 19B, © David Guttenfelder/AP Photo; 20T, © Takeshi Ishikawa/Polaris; 20B, © Aprilflower7/Shutterstock; 21, © Geoff A. Howard/Alamy; 22, © Takeshi Ishikawa/Polaris; 23T, © Takeshi Ishikawa/Polaris; 23B, © Julie DeGuia/Shutterstock; 24, © David Guttenfelder/AP Photo; 25T, © Kyodo/Newscom; 25B, © Takeshi Ishikawa/Polaris; 26, © jeremy sutton-hibbert/Alamy; 27T, Wikimedia/Public Domain; 27B, © Pierre Boutier/Polaris/Newscom; 28, © Kyodo via AP Images; 29, © Toru Takahashi/AP Photo; 31, © suatcan/Shutterstock.

Publisher: Kenn Goin
Senior Editor: Joyce Tavolacci
Creative Director: Spencer Brinker
Photo Research: Editorial Directions, Inc.

Library of Congress Cataloging-in-Publication Data

Names: Goldish, Meish, author.
Title: Toxic water : Minamata, Japan / by Meish Goldish.
Description: New York, New York : Bearport Publishing, [2018] | Series: Eco-disasters | Audience: Age 5–8. | Includes bibliographical references and index.
Identifiers: LCCN 2017010896 (print) | LCCN 2017011720 (ebook) | ISBN 9781684022786 (ebook) | ISBN 9781684022243 (library)
Subjects: LCSH: Mercury—Toxicology—Japan—Minamata-shi—Juvenile literature. | Water—Pollution—Japan—Minamata-shi—Juvenile literature.
Classification: LCC RA1231.M5 (ebook) | LCC RA1231.M5 G64 2018 (print) | DDC 615.9/25663095225—dc23
LC record available at https://lccn.loc.gov/2017010896

For more information, write to Bearport Publishing Company, Inc., 45 West 21st Street, Suite 3B, New York, New York 10010. Printed in the United States of America.

10 9 8 7 6 5 4 3 2 1

Contents

A Strange Disease

In April 1956 in Minamata, Japan, five-year-old Shizuko Tanaka sat down to eat with her family. As she stuck her chopsticks into a bowl of food, her tiny fingers began to tremble. By the next morning, Shizuko was seriously ill. The little girl was unable to walk, speak, or see, and her whole body shook wildly. Shizuko's mother rushed her to the hospital, but the doctors had no idea what was wrong. Two days later, Shizuko's little sister, Jitsuko, came down with the same terrifying **symptoms**.

The city of Minamata is located along Japan's southwestern coast.

A Japanese family eating a meal together

Shizuko's mother told the doctors that her neighbor's child had a similar illness. The doctors **investigated**. They soon found eight more people with the same symptoms. The hospital director reported that "an unknown disease of the **central nervous system**" had spread in Minamata. Everyone was puzzled—what could be causing this horrible illness?

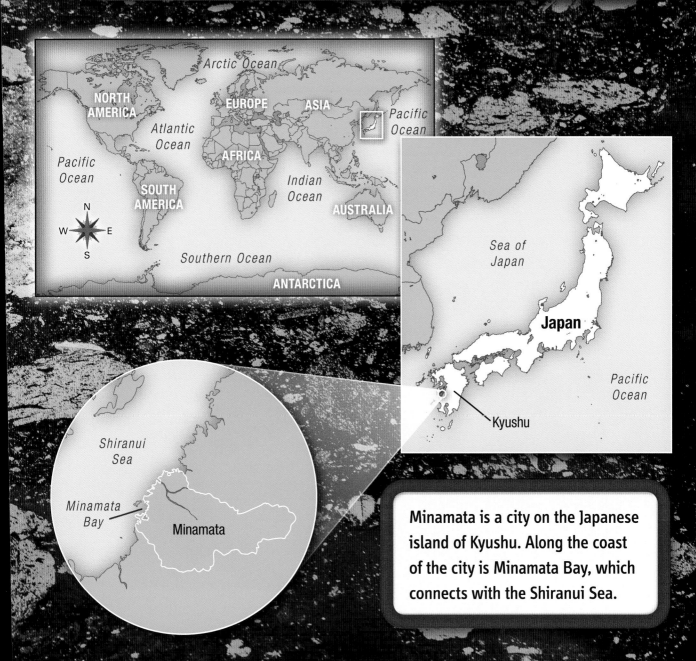

Minamata is a city on the Japanese island of Kyushu. Along the coast of the city is Minamata Bay, which connects with the Shiranui Sea.

Clues to the Mystery

Doctors in Minamata hunted for clues to explain the disease. They soon made some startling discoveries. **Residents** told them that before their loved ones became ill, cats in the area started behaving oddly. Some shrieked in pain, bumped into walls, or **convulsed** in the streets before dying. Others leapt into Minamata Bay, where they drowned. Residents called it "dancing cat disease."

Cats in Japan

The people of Minamata had also seen crows **plummet** from the sky or crash into rocks. What was also strange were the hundreds of dead fish floating in Minamata Bay. Fish and **shellfish** were a big part of the residents' diet. Cats and birds ate the seafood, too. Doctors soon realized that the sick people and animals had one thing in common—they had all eaten seafood that came from the bay.

A dead crow on a beach

Small fish that have died

Japanese seaweed

Fish and shellfish weren't the only things that died in Minamata Bay. Investigators found that seaweed in the water had also stopped growing and died.

More Signs of Sickness

By October of 1956, the number of people known to have the strange disease had increased to 54. Doctors now had a name for the illness—Minamata disease. Sadly, 17 of those **victims** died not long after seeking medical help. Panic spread throughout Minamata. Healthy residents feared that they, or their families, might get sick and die. The serious situation led **researchers** from a nearby university to join the doctors in studying the illness.

A fisher in Minamata

Many victims of Minamata disease were fishers who caught, sold, and ate fish and shellfish from Minamata Bay.

A fisher prepares a meal of seafood.

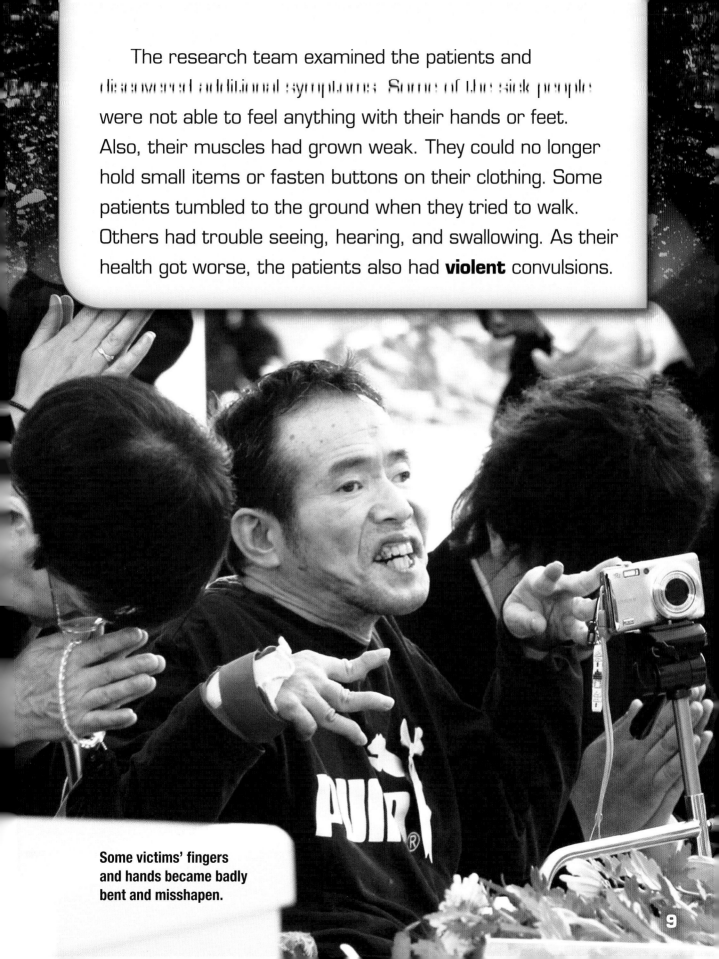

The research team examined the patients and discovered additional symptoms. Some of the sick people were not able to feel anything with their hands or feet. Also, their muscles had grown weak. They could no longer hold small items or fasten buttons on their clothing. Some patients tumbled to the ground when they tried to walk. Others had trouble seeing, hearing, and swallowing. As their health got worse, the patients also had **violent** convulsions.

Some victims' fingers and hands became badly bent and misshapen.

Finding a Killer

As Minamata disease spread, the hunt for its cause continued. The research team knew that all the victims had eaten fish and shellfish from Minamata Bay. They **suspected** that the seafood had poisoned the victims. If so, then what had poisoned the fish and shellfish?

Seafood is a main part of the diet for most people living in Minamata.

The researchers began testing the water in Minamata Bay. The results were shocking. They found that it held high amounts of an extremely poisonous **chemical** called methyl mercury. The chemical **contaminated** fish and other living things before eventually killing them. When people and animals ate the fish, they, too, were poisoned by methyl mercury.

The water in Minamata Bay was tested for different chemicals.

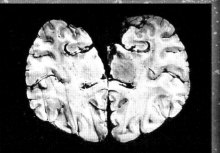

Methyl mercury has **toxic** effects on the brain and other parts of the central nervous system. It destroys brain cells and can kill a victim within weeks or over a period of years.

The top brain is filled with holes as a result of methyl mercury poisoning. The larger brain belongs to a healthy adult.

Toxic Wastewater

In 1959, the researchers announced that methyl mercury poisoning was the cause of Minamata disease. Yet one mystery still remained: How did the methyl mercury get into Minamata Bay? Researchers found the highest levels of the dangerous chemical in the water near a factory. The large business was run by a company called the Chisso Corporation.

Minamata Bay in spring

The Chisso factory made chemicals that were used to **manufacture** plastics. One of the **by-products** was methyl mercury! Researchers soon discovered how poison had gotten into Minamata Bay. The factory was dumping its methyl mercury-filled wastewater into the bay. Over the years, the poison had built up and contaminated the water.

The Chisso factory in Minamata

The Chisso factory opened in 1908, yet people didn't start to get Minamata disease until the 1950s. That's because in 1951 the company changed the way it made plastics, which created the deadly methyl mercury.

Keeping Silent

When the research team brought their findings to the Chisso Corporation, the company refused to take responsibility. They denied that methyl mercury from their factory was causing Minamata disease. Even more disturbing, the company continued to dump its toxic wastewater into the bay.

In the 1950s, the Chisso factory was considered one of the most modern factories in all of Japan.

Unfortunately, the Japanese government did nothing to stop Chisso at the time. Why? The company had created many jobs for local people. In fact, one out of every four workers in the city was employed by Chisso. Also, the company was a successful business that brought in a lot of money. This helped Japan's **economy** to grow. The government didn't want to do anything that might hurt its own economy and Chisso's business—even if that meant allowing people to be harmed.

A resident of Minamata looks out over the water.

Many people in Minamata were afraid to speak out against Chisso. They feared losing their jobs.

Angry Fishers

The methyl mercury in Minamata Bay didn't just make people sick. It also put fishers out of work. There was little seafood to catch in the bay, since the poisoned wastewater had killed most of the fish and shellfish. Fishers had a hard time selling the few items they did catch because it was unsafe to eat.

Fishers haul in empty nets. By the 1960s, business for Minamata fishers had dropped by 91 percent.

After being silent for years, the fishers and others affected by the disease had finally had enough. In 1959, some 1,500 people forced their way into the Chisso factory and **rioted**. They were so angry they tried to tear apart the factory with their bare hands. The rioters demanded that the company pay for their lost earnings. Without admitting guilt, Chisso agreed to pay a total of about $250,000—but only to a small group impacted by the disease. Considering all that the people had lost, the money was little more than a **token**.

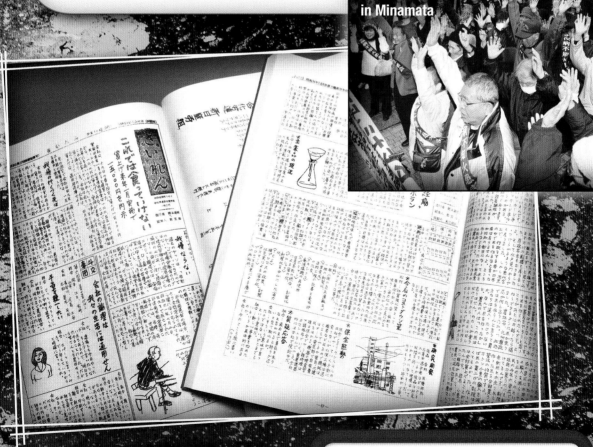

A group of protesters in Minamata

Chisso factory workers recorded their concerns about Minamata disease in these journals.

In October 1959, one of the Minamata hospital doctors proved that polluted water from the bay had given a cat Minamata disease.

Fighting for Justice

News of the fishers' **protest** spread throughout Japan. As more people got sick and died, their families and other members of the community joined in. Some victims even camped outside the Chisso factory. Victims' families demanded that Chisso pay them for their medical bills, losses, and suffering.

Minamata victims and their families protest together.

Masazumi Harada, a Japanese doctor and researcher, agreed with the people. He said, "Minamata disease is the result of **criminal** acts by a corporation and the government." In 1959, Chisso began paying victims. Each adult received only $278 and each child was given $83 per year. In addition, families of victims who had died received just $889.

Many people wrongly believed that Minamata disease was **contagious**. They avoided anyone they thought might be sick. Ogata Masato, a fisher, said, "People stopped seeing their fellow humans as human beings."

Dr. Masazumi Harada treats a patient with Minamata disease.

Many victims of Minamata disease were isolated from the community. Store workers refused to touch customers they feared might have Minamata disease.

More Pollution

Even after paying disease victims, the Chisso factory continued to dump its **polluted** wastewater into Minamata Bay. In 1960, the company's production of methyl mercury actually increased. Eventually, the deadly pollution spread to the Shiranui Sea. As a result, more and more people got Minamata disease and died.

Wastewater from the Chisso factory

The Shiranui Sea

In 1965, things got even worse. Minamata disease struck another Japanese city called Niigata. An electrical company called Showa Denko ran a chemical factory there. It, too, was dumping mercury-filled wastewater into a nearby river, sickening the local people. The Japanese government finally took action. In 1968, the government declared that Chisso's poisoned wastewater was the cause of Minamata disease. It ordered the factory to stop dumping methyl mercury into the bay and sea. Showa Denko, too, was eventually held responsible for polluting the water.

The Japanese city of Niigata

Showa Denko, like Chisso, ended up paying Minamata disease victims and their families for their suffering.

Mother to Child

Even after Japan **banned** the dumping of poisoned wastewater, new cases of Minamata disease appeared. Surprisingly, many of the younger victims had never eaten the poisoned fish and seafood. Then how did they get sick?

Children suffering from Minamata disease receive therapy at a special clinic.

In the 1950s and 1960s when the methyl mercury poisoning was at its worst, many women ate contaminated seafood. However, they had no idea their bodies were being poisoned. Why? Many showed no signs of the disease. A large number of these women went on to have children. While pregnant, the mothers' poisoned blood was passed on to their babies. The mercury had a huge effect on the tiny babies' developing bodies and brains. Even before they were born, the babies were victims of Minimata disease.

A mother holds her child, who has Minamata disease.

Babies born to mothers who had eaten contaminated seafood often had brain damage and their bodies were badly misshapen.

Methyl mercury is one of the few poisonous chemicals that can enter an unborn baby through its mother's blood.

After 60 Years

After 60 years, the effects of Minamata disease are still being felt in Japan. Jitsuko Tanaka and her sister Shizuko were two of the first victims to develop Minamata disease. Jitsuko was just two years old at the time. The disease left her unable to speak. Her last words as a child were "I cannot put on my shoes." Shizuko died three years after she fell ill, but Jitsuko survived.

Victims of Minamata disease often cannot care for themselves. Some need help with the most basic tasks, such as eating.

Today, Jitsuko is in her 60s. She lives with another sister, Ayako, and her brother-in-law, Yoshio. Like a small child, Jitsuko needs 24-hour care. The only sound she makes is a soft hum. Several times a day, she performs a strange act. She squats down and turns in circles on her knees. Sometimes, Jitsuko goes days without sleeping. Often her body shakes uncontrollably. Her sister Ayako worries. "Who is going to care for Jitsuko after we pass away?"

These victims of Minamata disease celebrate turning 60 years old.

Jitsuko Tanaka as a child

Jitsuko's brother-in-law Yoshio says, "I would like people to know that Jitsuko is one of the first who fell ill and that she is still alive."

Minamata Today

Victims like Jitsuko are living reminders that the problems caused by the disease haven't gone away. Many patients are **confined** to wheelchairs or beds and cannot care for themselves. Their families continue to sue Chisso and the Japanese government for more help.

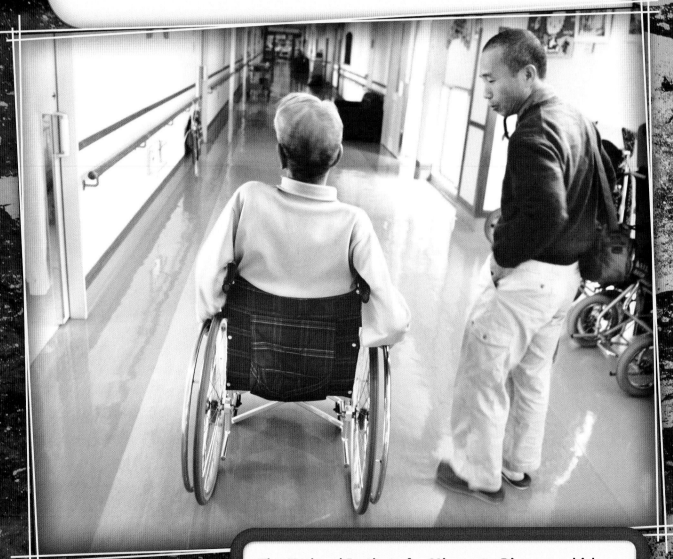

A Minamata disease victim in a wheelchair

The National Institute for Minamata Disease, which is part of the Japanese government, does research on the illness and the environment. It also teaches people around the world about what happened in Minamata.

Groups around Japan, such as Hotto Hausu, are working to help the victims and also to raise awareness about the **tragedy**. Members provide job training for victims and teach people about Minamata disease. This group and others affected by the disease are fighting to keep Japan and the world safe from another **devastating** chemical crisis. "We now need to relay the Minamata story to future generations," one member says.

A memorial was built in Japan to honor the victims of Minamata disease.

These people march to raise awareness about Minamata disease and industrial pollution.

Fixing the Future

Since the Minamata disaster occurred, actions have been taken to prevent methyl mercury poisoning from happening in the future. Here are some examples.

The Minamata Convention on Mercury

The Minamata Convention on Mercury is a global agreement between members of the United Nations to protect human health and the environment from the damaging effects of mercury. The agreement became international law on August 16, 2017, and includes four key actions:

1. Lower the amount of mercury used in industry throughout the world.
2. Replace mercury with new, safer chemicals.
3. Clean up the mercury that has already been dumped into the environment.
4. Stop buying or selling mercury in order to prevent mercury pollution.

Stopping Mercury Poisoning Worldwide

Since the Minamata environmental disaster occurred, other cases of methyl mercury poisoning have been discovered. People around the world are fighting to stop methyl mercury poisoning and pollution.

- In Indonesia, groups are working to get the government to ban the use of mercury in gold mining. Mine workers have gotten illnesses similar to Minamata disease. Victims of Minamata disease have traveled to Indonesia to speak on behalf of all sufferers of mercury poisoning.

- First Nations people in Canada have also been affected by mercury pollution from factory waste. Researchers from the Japanese National Institute for Minamata Disease have traveled to Canada over the past 40 years to help the victims.

The Minamata Convention at the United Nations

Victim Advocates

- Many individuals work as **advocates** for victims and teach people about Minamata disease. One advocate is Yuta Jitsukawa. He heads an organization called Minamata Forum. It presents programs where both researchers and victims take part in talks with young people in Japan.

- Another advocate is Dr. Tatsuaki Okamoto. He wrote a six-volume, 3,700-page work called *People's History of Minamata Disease*. His goal is to present the disease's history through the voices of its victims.

- Yoshiko Shiotani, a former governor, talks about Minamata disease to college students and other residents of Tokyo. She says, "I believe an examination of our experiences of Minamata will be helpful for developing countries." Yoshiko also helps children who got the disease through their mother's poisoned blood. "It is shameful that the Minamata issue has not been solved in 60 years," she says.

A victim of Minamata disease speaks out.

Glossary

advocates (AD-vuh-kits) people who support or speak in favor of something

banned (BAND) did not allow

by-products (BYE-prod-uhkts) things that are left over after you make something

central nervous system (SEN-truhl NUR-vuhss SISS-tuhm) a person's or animal's brain and spinal cord, which control the body's movement and activities

chemical (KEM-uh-kuhl) a natural or man-made substance

confined (kuhn-FINED) limited to

contagious (kuhn-TAY-juhss) able to be passed from person to person

contaminated (kuhn-TAM-uh-nay-tid) polluted or unfit for use

convulsed (kuhn-VULSD) shook uncontrollably

criminal (KRIH-min-uhl) having to do with breaking the law

devastating (DEV-uh-stay-ting) damaging or very upsetting

economy (i-KON-uh-mee) the way a country runs its industry, trade, and finance

investigated (in-VESS-tuh-gate-uhd) found out about something

manufacture (man-yuh-FAK-chur) to make something, often with machines

plummet (PLUHM-it) to drop suddenly

polluted (puh-LOOT-uhd) damaged by harmful waste or chemicals

protest (PROH-test) an organized gathering in which people express their disagreement

researchers (REE-sur-churz) people who study things or collect information

residents (REZ-uh-duhnss) people who live in a particular place

rioted (RHY-uh-tid) came together in a disorderly public gathering

shellfish (SHEL-fish) sea creatures, such as crabs and clams, that live in water and have a hard outer shell

suspected (suh-SPEK-tid) thought that something may be true

symptoms (SIMP-tuhmz) signs of a disease

token (TOH-kuhn) a symbolic gesture

toxic (TOHK-sik) poisonous or deadly

tragedy (TRAJ-uh-dee) a sad and terrible event

victims (VIK-tuhmz) people or animals that have been hurt or killed by someone or something

violent (VHY-uh-luhnt) with uncontrolled force

Bibliography

Harada, Masazumi. *Minamata Disease.* Tokyo: Minamata Disease Patients Alliance (2004).

Hernan, Robert Emmet. *This Borrowed Earth: Lessons from the 15 Worst Environmental Disasters Around the World.* New York: Palgrave Macmillan (2010).

Ishimure, Michiko. *Paradise in the Sea of Sorrow: Our Minamata Disease.* Ann Arbor, MI: University of Michigan Center for Japanese Studies (2003).

Keibo, Oiwa. *Rowing the Eternal Sea: The Story of a Minamata Fisherman.* Lanham, MD: Rowman & Littlefield (2001).

Read More

Lawrence, Ellen. *Polluted Oceans (Green World, Clean World).* New York: Bearport (2014).

Simons, Rae. *A Kid's Guide to Pollution and How It Can Make You Sick.* Vestal, NY: Village Earth Press (2016).

Learn More Online

To learn more about toxic water in Minamata, Japan, visit
www.bearportpublishing.com/EcoDisasters

Index

About the Author

Meish Goldish has written more than 300 books for children. His book *City Firefighters* won a Teachers' Choice Award in 2015. He lives in Brooklyn, New York.